Bicycling Adventures

by Karen and Glen Bledsoe

Consultant:
Daniel D'Ambrosio
Editor
Adventure Cycling Association

CAPSTONE
HIGH-INTEREST
BOOKS

an imprint of Capstone Press
Mankato, Minnesota

Capstone High-Interest Books are published by Capstone Press
151 Good Counsel Drive, P.O. Box 669, Mankato, Minnesota 56002
http://www.capstone-press.com

Library of Congress Cataloging-in-Publication Data
Bledsoe, Karen E.
    Bicycling adventures/by Karen and Glen Bledsoe.
    p. cm.—(Dangerous adventures)
    Includes bibliographical references and index. (p.48)
    ISBN 0-7368-0904-X
    1. Bicycle touring—History—Juvenile literature. [1. Bicycle touring.] I. Bledsoe,
Glen. II. Title. III. Series.
GV1044 .B57 2002
796.6'4—dc21   00-012701

Summary: Describes adventures in riding bicycles, including a history of bicycles and
the adventures of long-distance cyclists.

Editorial Credits
Tom Adamson, editor; Lois Wallentine, product planning editor; Heather Kindseth,
    cover designer; Timothy Halldin, production designer; Katy Kudela,
    photo researcher

Photo Credits
Bicycle Museum of America, 10, 12, 14, 16
Dan Buettner, 4, 7, 32, 34, 37, 38, 40
Geoff Thorpe, 28
http://www.pennyfarthingworldtour.com, 43
Karen E. Martin, cover, 18, 20, 23
Larry Savage, 8, 26

Table of Contents

Chapter 1

Bicycling Adventures

In August 1993, four men rode their bicycles onto Cape Agulhas in South Africa. They had been riding 262 days. They began their trip in Tunisia in northern Africa. They had ridden through hot deserts and wet forests. They had endured injuries and serious illness. On Cape Agulhas, the cyclists celebrated the end of a journey of 11,855 miles (19,078 kilometers). They had bicycled from one end of Africa to the other.

Long-Distance Bicycling
Every year, hundreds of cyclists go on long-distance adventures. They ride across

Dan Buettner and his team cycled across Africa in 1992–1993.

one or more countries. Some cyclists even ride around the world. These cyclists may take an airplane or boat across oceans.

People have different reasons for planning long-distance rides. Some long-distance cyclists ride for a charity. They hope people who hear about their adventure will give money to the charity they support.

Most long-distance cyclists travel for fun. They want to see what life is like in other countries. They want to meet new people and learn about the world.

Planning for Safety

Long-distance cyclists must plan carefully. They study the countries where they will travel. They read traveler's guidebooks, cycling magazines, and information on the Internet. This information must be current and correct.

Cyclists can face dangers in any country. Fast-moving cars and trucks can accidentally hit them. Cyclists also must be careful about riding in bad weather. Rain can make roads slippery. Cyclists always should wear helmets while riding.

Long-distance cyclists carry their gear in nylon bags called panniers.

Supplies and Equipment

Long-distance cyclists carry almost all of their equipment. Some cyclists mail spare bicycle parts to cities on their travel route. Cyclists carry tools to repair their bicycles. They carry repair kits to patch flat tires. Cyclists pack gear in panniers. These nylon bags hang over the sides of the bicycle. Bicycles must be sturdy to carry this equipment.

Many cyclists carry camping gear. Camping is less expensive than staying in hotels. Cyclists can set up tents anywhere they have permission to camp. Some tents are big enough to put the bicycles inside. Cyclists also carry small gas stoves for cooking.

In some areas, clean drinking water is hard to find. Cyclists may carry water purification tablets or water filters. These items make water clean enough to drink.

Cyclists also carry first aid kits. The kits should include bandages, tape, scissors, a pocket knife, and pain reliever.

Cyclists carry maps. But they sometimes ask for directions from local people. They carry books to help them understand a few words of the local language.

Some cyclists carry laptop computers. They use the computers to send e-mail. They may post journals and photos on Web sites. People throughout the world can read about the cyclists' adventures.

Long-distance cyclists carry their trash with them until they can dispose of it.

Chapter 2

Famous Firsts

The first picture of a bicycle-like machine appears in one of Leonardo da Vinci's sketchbooks. Da Vinci was a famous artist. He lived in Italy during the 1400s. His drawing looks like a modern bicycle. But da Vinci probably never built the machine.

The First Bicycles

In 1839, a man in Scotland named Kirkpatrick MacMillan invented the first true bicycle. Riders put their feet on levers. The levers pulled rods that turned the back wheel. MacMillan's invention did not become popular.

In the 1860s, Pierre Michaux and his son Ernest built a bicycle with pedals on the front

Penny-farthings had a large front wheel and a small rear wheel.

Pierre and Ernest Michaux built a machine called a velocipede.

wheel. They called the machine a velocipede. The velocipede could not go very fast. The pedals were attached to the front wheel. The velocipede could only go as fast as the rider turned the pedals.

Inventors made the front wheel larger to increase speed. These machines were the first to be called bicycles. They were nicknamed penny-farthings because the front wheel was much larger than the back wheel. The English coin called a farthing is much smaller than the English penny. An English inventor named James Starley is credited with inventing this bicycle in 1871.

Around the World

In the 1880s, an English man named Thomas Stevens rode a penny-farthing bicycle around the world. He sent letters about his travels to a magazine called *Outing*. The magazine published his letters.

Stevens began his trip in San Francisco. There were few roads in western North America at the time. Stevens had to ride on trails or along railroad tracks. He carried no food or supplies with him. He stayed at farmhouses and hotels along the way.

Stevens became famous by the time he arrived in Europe. After leaving Europe, his trip became more dangerous. He was attacked by sheep dogs in the Middle East. He encountered bandits in the Caucasus Mountains

The Rover Safety bicycle was the first bicycle to have a chain drive.

in Russia. He had to wave a hand gun to keep them away.

Stevens ended his trip in Tokyo. He was the first person to cycle around the world. He also was the first person to cycle across the United States, across Europe, and across Asia.

Bicycle Improvements

In the 1880s, bicycles with chain drives were invented. A chain connects the pedals to the rear wheel. The chain turns a gear. The gear makes the bicycle easier to pedal. The Rover Safety bicycle was a popular model. Safety bicycles made cycling more popular than ever.

The air-filled tire was another important improvement. Early bicycles had metal or wooden wheels with hard rubber tires. Scottish veterinarian John Dunlop invented a rubber tire filled with air. This type of tire is called a pneumatic tire. Bicycles with Dunlop tires allowed cyclists to go faster. Air-filled tires also gave cyclists a smoother ride.

Across the United States

In August 1895, George Loher rode his bicycle across the United States. He rode a Stearns Yellow Fellow bicycle. This bicycle had no brakes. Loher had to drag his feet on the ground or put his shoe on a wheel to slow down and stop.

MacMillan's bicycle had levers and rods that turned the back wheel.

Loher began his trip in Oakland, California. The western United States had few roads. What roads existed often were muddy or covered with several inches of dust. Loher often rode on railroad tracks.

Loher carried no food. Farming families usually let him sleep in their homes. They cooked meals for him. When in a town, Loher stayed in a hotel.

Loher knew how to fix flat tires. But other parts of his bicycle sometimes needed repairs. He sometimes had to tie parts together with wire or twine. Blacksmiths helped him fix broken parts. These workers make and fix things made of iron.

In the eastern United States, Loher rode along canals. People used these channels of water to transport cargo on barges. The barges were flat boats that were towed by mules. The mules walked on a path by the canal. Loher rode on these paths. The barge owners did not like this. They thought his bicycle scared the mules.

Loher rode into New York City on October 30. He had bicycled more than 4,000 miles (6,400 kilometers).

Chapter 3

From Alaska to Argentina

Many bicyclists today enjoy long-distance challenges. They ride across countries or across continents. B.J. and Karen Martin rode from Alaska to Argentina. They traveled the length of North and South America.

A Difficult Start

The Martins flew to Prudhoe Bay, Alaska. On June 1, 1995, they began their ride from the town of Deadhorse. On the first night, the temperature dropped below freezing. They broke a tent pole while trying to set up a tent.

The next day, B.J.'s bicycle chain slipped off. He saw that the front chainring was bent.

B.J. and Karen Martin began their bicycling adventure in 1995.

The Martins often had to ride on rough, unpaved roads.

This gear holds the chain. The Martins pushed their bicycles down the gravel highway to a campground. B.J. checked a repair manual. He read that the chainring was almost impossible to repair. He took it apart anyway and tapped it gently with a hammer. He was able to fix the chainring.

Canada and the United States

The Martins cycled south through Canada. In August, they crossed the U.S. border and entered Montana. They stayed at campgrounds. They crossed Idaho and cycled across Oregon. They rode down the West Coast through rain and fog. They had a hard time keeping dry. They had to stop at every laundromat they found to dry their clothing.

The Martins continued riding south along the West Coast. They stayed with friends in San Diego for a month. They repaired their bicycles and equipment. They rested before continuing their journey.

Mexico

The Martins next crossed the Mexican border. Karen knew some Spanish. She was able to communicate with the Mexican people they met.

The Martins worried about finding clean drinking water. Their maps showed long distances between villages. But they frequently encountered villages. The villages had clean water. The Martins realized that their maps were inaccurate.

The Martins rode through desert areas in Baja. They found truck stops along the way. The truck stops were small, open structures attached to the owner's house. The people there served good food. They were friendly and often offered to let the Martins stay in their houses overnight.

The Martins Get Sick
The Martins reached Guatemala by the end of January, 1996. They rode in the morning to avoid the heat of the day. But they tired easily in the heat and humidity. They began to feel sick. They went to a doctor. Tests showed they did not have any diseases. They continued on to El Salvador.

In El Salvador, the Martins were still sick. They nearly collapsed on the road. They went to see a doctor in the city of San Salvador. The doctor said that they were not getting enough vitamins and minerals. They needed more calories. They rested and took large doses of vitamins. They ate good food until they felt better.

South America
The Martins rode to Copacabana, Bolivia. The church in the town has a tradition of blessing vehicles. The Martins took part in the ceremony. They saw that people had decorated

The Martins dipped their bicycles' wheels in Lake Titicaca as part of a ceremony in Bolivia.

cars they wanted blessed. The Martins decorated their bicycles with streamers. People told them to light firecrackers underneath the bicycles. Part of the ceremony is to dip the wheels in Lake Titicaca.

The Martins left Copacabana and continued riding through Bolivia. When a storm threatened, they took shelter in a village schoolhouse. The children were curious about the bicycles and the riders. The Martins showed them how bicycles work. They used their maps to teach a geography lesson. They showed the children the route they had been traveling. The Martins gave the children the last of their paper and pens as a gift.

Argentina

The Martins rode into Argentina and across the Pampas. These broad, grassy plains cover much of Argentina. In December 1996, they reached the Patagonia region. The strong winds there knocked them off their bicycles. They took shelter in Perito Moreno. A man who ran a campground urged them to stay. Christmas was just a few days away. The Martins stayed in the campground.

The Martins continued through Patagonia. But gusty winds continued to knock them off their bicycles. They reached the southern tip of Patagonia and took a ferry to Tierra del Fuego. These islands are located at the southern tip of South America. The Martins cycled across the islands and completed their journey on January 11, 1997. They had ridden about 18,000 miles (29,000 kilometers) in 19 months.

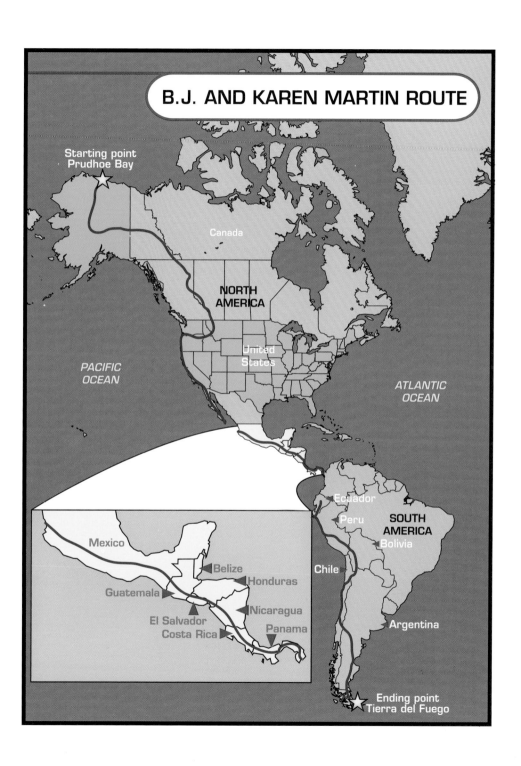

B.J. AND KAREN MARTIN ROUTE

Starting point
Prudhoe Bay

Canada

PACIFIC
OCEAN

NORTH
AMERICA

United
States

ATLANTIC
OCEAN

Ecuador

Peru

SOUTH
AMERICA

Bolivia

Chile

Mexico

Belize

Honduras

Guatemala

El Salvador

Nicaragua

Costa Rica

Panama

Argentina

Ending point
Tierra del Fuego

Chapter 4

Bicycling Around the World

In May, 1978, Barbara and Larry Savage began their around-the-world bicycle adventure in California. They were not experienced bicyclists. When they began their trip, they carried too much gear. They mailed home much of the extra clothing they had packed.

The beginning of the trip was difficult. Cycling up steep hills in the hot sun was tiring. They were not used to riding bicycles loaded with gear.

They slowly rode north to Canada. They then rode east across the United States. The Savages eventually reached Florida. There they visited with relatives.

Larry and Barbara Savage cycled through several different countries during their bicycling adventure.

The Savages encountered crowded roads in India.

Europe

The Savages flew from Florida to Spain. They rested in Spain until spring. They rode through Spain, then traveled to Morocco. Morocco's roads were very rough. The weather was hot.

After Morocco, the Savages toured the British Isles. They enjoyed the smooth roads and friendly people. They liked being able to communicate in English.

The Savages continued cycling in France. While riding into Paris, Barbara began to feel strange vibrations coming from her bicycle's front fork. This part holds the front wheel. Her bicycle became hard to steer. She told Larry about the vibrations. He thought she was imagining the shaking. He decided to test her bicycle himself. He grabbed her bike and jumped on. He rode a few feet and the bike collapsed. They could have been seriously injured if the bicycle had collapsed in traffic or while riding downhill.

Egypt

In October 1979, the Savages reached Cairo, Egypt. Their trip through Egypt was very difficult. Roads were very dusty. Flies and gnats filled the air.

People in small villages stared at the Savages with curiosity. These people had never before seen Americans on bicycles with huge packs of gear. Some Egyptians were not friendly and threw stones at them.

Asia

Bicycling in India's heavy traffic was difficult. Buses, cars, trucks, carts, and cows crowded the highways in New Delhi. Near Kanpur, bicyclists going home from work crowded the highway. An Indian bicyclist crashed into Larry. Larry fell and broke his wrist and cracked his ribs. He continued cycling in pain.

In Nepal, much of the food was spoiled by germs. In one town, the Savages saw food being prepared on the dirty front steps of an inn. Mice ran on the food. Drinking water had worms in it. Dead mice and manure filled the streets of many of the small towns. Some of the food they ate made them sick. But the Savages found many restaurants that served good food in the capital city of Kathmandu.

New Zealand

The Savages were happy to return to smooth roads when they cycled through New Zealand. But they encountered very strong winds. They were blown off their bicycles. Barbara began walking her bicycle. But the wind nearly blew it out of her hands.

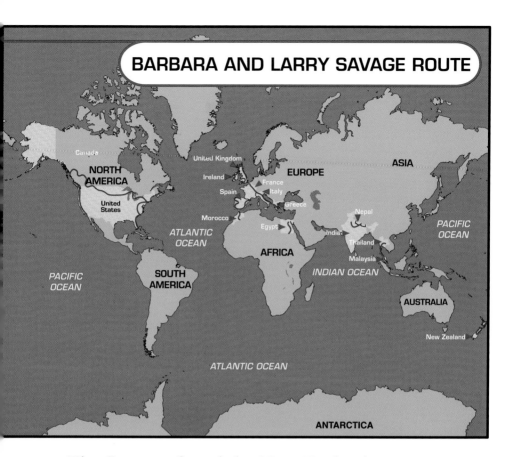

BARBARA AND LARRY SAVAGE ROUTE

The Savages found the New Zealanders to be the friendliest people in the world. People often invited them to stay at their houses or give them rides if it was raining. The Savages often had to stay up all night talking with their friendly hosts.

In April 1980, the Savages flew back to Los Angeles after nearly two years of cycling. They had bicycled more than 22,500 miles (36,200 kilometers).

Chapter 5

A Career Adventurer

For most adventure cyclists, a trip around the world or across a continent is a once-in-a-lifetime adventure. For Dan Buettner, adventure cycling has become a career. Buettner cycled from Alaska to Argentina in 1986 and 1987. Since then, he has gone on many long-distance trips.

Sovietrek
In 1990, Buettner and a team of cyclists rode across the United States, Europe, and the Soviet Union. The Soviet Union was a large union of republics in Eastern Europe and Asia. In 1991, the government of the Soviet Union

In 1990, Dan and Steve Buettner and two Soviet citizens took part in Sovietrek.

Long-distance cyclists do not always ride in perfect road conditions.

collapsed. The Union broke apart into Russia and other smaller nations.

The Soviet Union and the United States had not been friendly toward each other. But in 1990, relations between the United States and the Soviet Union were improving.

Buettner called his adventure Sovietrek. He put together a team of four riders. Buettner invited his brother Steve and two Soviet citizens to join him.

The team began Sovietrek in St. Paul, Minnesota, on April 1, 1990. The cyclists rode to New York City. The group then took a plane to France. They cycled through Europe and reached the border of the Soviet Union on June 4, 1990. They spent 124 days cycling across the Soviet Union. They often stayed overnight with Russians in their homes.

The Buettners had to eat foods they had never seen before. Steve Buettner ate food he did not know was spoiled with salmonella bacteria. He came down with salmonella poisoning. His body temperature rose to 105 degrees Fahrenheit (41 degrees Celsius). Normal body temperature is 98.6 degrees Fahrenheit (37 degrees Celsius). He had to stay in a hospital for a week before he was well enough to ride again.

In October, the team reached Vladivostok. This city is on Russia's eastern coast by the Sea of Japan. They had bicycled 7,353 miles (11,833 kilometers) across the Soviet Union.

The team then flew back to the United
States. They cycled 2,200 miles (3,540
kilometers) from Los Angeles back to St. Paul.
The entire trip took 239 days. The team cycled
12,888 miles (20,741 kilometers).

Africatrek

In 1992 and 1993, Buettner and a team of
cyclists rode the length of the African
continent. Buettner's brother Steve again
rode with him.

The Buettners made the trip into an
educational experience for students around
the world. They planned to post messages
on the Internet. People at a university in
Minnesota helped them prepare educational
packets for schools.

The Africatrek team began their ride
in Tunisia. This country borders the
Mediterranean Sea.

The team rode across Algeria and into the
Sahara Desert. They knew that some areas had
only a wide band of wheel tracks instead of

The Africatrek team had to protect themselves from blowing sand in the Sahara Desert.

roads. There were no sources of water. After two days, the team realized that riding bicycles across the Sahara was too dangerous. Their water supply was running low. They turned around and rode out of the desert. They then flew to Niger. From there they bicycled through Nigeria and into Zaire.

Team members began to get sick. They had malaria, diarrhea, and intestinal worms. In

Uganda, they found a restaurant and ate a large meal. They began to feel better. But they were still weak from disease. The team rested and recovered from their illnesses.

The team had fewer problems riding through Tanzania. The Buettners stopped along the way to climb Mount Kilamanjaro. The team then crossed into Mozambique. This country was damaged by years of civil war. The road the team wanted to travel was nicknamed "Machine Gun Alley." United Nations peacekeeping forces helped them through this area.

After crossing Zimbabwe, the cyclists entered South Africa. The city of Johannesburg is much like cities in North America. It was a major contrast to the rest of Africa. From Johannesburg, the team continued south to the coast.

On August 17, 1993, the team reached Cape Agulhas. This spot is the southernmost tip of the African continent. The Africatrek journey was finished. It had taken 262 days to complete the 11,855-mile (19,078-kilometer) ride.

The Africatrek team crossed wooden bridges in Zaire.

Chapter 6

Adventure Bicycling Today

Many people have ridden around the world on their own. They had to make all their own plans. They encountered dangers and hardships.

Some groups organize world bicycle tours. People pay for the costs of the tours. The organization makes all the plans for the entire group. They arrange for overnight stays and buy everyone's food.

Interactive Adventures

Dan Buettner is now part of a company called Classroom Connect. He leads interactive expeditions called "Quests." He bicycles through different parts of the world. He

The Buettners now go on Quests to various parts of the world to solve ancient mysteries.

sends messages to an Internet site. Students can read about his adventures and help decide what areas he and his team explore. The Quest teams often study mysteries about ancient civilizations.

For MayaQuest, Buettner's team bicycled through Guatemala, Belize, and the Yucatán region of Mexico. They studied Mayan culture. The Maya lived there before Europeans arrived. The Mayan culture mysteriously began to decline more than 1,000 years ago.

AmericaQuest took a team through the Colorado Plateaus. This area contains ruins of an ancient people called the Anasazi. These people made mud brick homes high on cliffs.

Buettner completed AustraliaQuest in fall 2000. The team studied Aboriginal culture.

An Individual Challenge

Jonathan Summerfield of England is planning an unusual long-distance adventure. He hopes to ride around the world on an old-fashioned high-wheeler bicycle. He calls his trip the Penny-Farthing World Tour.

Summerfield rode the length of Great Britain in 2000 to prepare for an around-the-world trip.

Summerfield hopes to re-create the same ride that Thomas Stevens took in the 1880s. His exact route will depend upon conditions in countries where he plans to travel. He does not plan to ride through countries that are at war. Summerfield planned to begin his journey in spring 2001.

Words to Know

blacksmith (BLAK-smith)—a person who makes and fixes things made of iron

chainring (CHAYN-ring)—the gear that holds the bicycle's chain

malaria (muh-LAIR-ee-ah)—a serious disease that people get from mosquito bites; malaria causes high fever, chills, and sometimes death.

panniers (PAN-yurz)—nylon bags that hang over the sides of a bicycle; long-distance bicyclists carry their gear in panniers.

pneumatic tire (noo-MAT-ik TIRE)—a hollow rubber tire that is filled with air

salmonella (sal-muh-NEL-uh)—a type of bacteria that can cause food poisoning

To Learn More

Ballentine, Richard. *Ultimate Bicycle Book.* New York: DK Publishing, 1998.

Buettner, Dan. *Africatrek: A Journey by Bicycle through Africa.* Minneapolis: Lerner, 1997.

Buettner, Dan. *Sovietrek: A Journey by Bicycle across Russia.* Minneapolis: Lerner, 1994.

Hayhurst, Chris. *Bike Trekking: Have Fun, Be Smart.* Explore the Outdoors. New York: Rosen, 2000.

Useful Addresses

Adventure Cycling Association
150 East Pine Street
P.O. Box 8308
Missoula, MT 59807

The Bicycle Museum of America
7 West Monroe Street
New Bremen, OH 45869

Canadian Cycling Association
702-2197 Riverside Drive
Suite 212A
Ottawa, ON K1H 7X3
Canada

League of American Bicyclists
1612 K Street NW
Suite 401
Washington, DC 20006-2082

Internet Sites

Adventure Cycling Association
http://www.adventurecycling.org

The Bicycle Museum of America
http://www.bicyclemuseum.com

Canadian Cycling Association
http://www.canadian-cycling.com

League of American Bicyclists
http://www.bikeleague.org

The Quest Channel
http://www.quest.classroom.com

Index